MOTORSPORTS MANIACS

DIRT TRACK RACING

BY KATE MIKOLEY

Gareth Stevens
PUBLISHING

Please visit our website, www.garethstevens.com. For a free color catalog of all our high-quality books, call toll free 1-800-542-2595 or fax 1-877-542-2596.

Cataloging-in-Publication Data

Names: Mikoley, Kate.
Title: Dirt Track Racing / Kate Mikoley.
Description: New York : Gareth Stevens Publishing, 2020. | Series: Motorsports maniacs | Includes glossary and index.
Identifiers: ISBN 9781538240823 (pbk.) | ISBN 9781538240847 (library bound) | ISBN 9781538240830 (6 pack)
Subjects: LCSH: Automobile racing on dirt--Juvenile literature. | Automobile racing--Juvenile literature.
Classification: LCC GV1029.9.D57 M55 2020 | DDC 796.72--dc23

First Edition

Published in 2020 by
Gareth Stevens Publishing
111 East 14th Street, Suite 349
New York, NY 10003

Designer: Sarah Liddell
Editor: Kate Mikoley

Photo credits: Cover, p. 1 Art Konovalov/Shutterstock.com; dirt background used throughout Yibo Wang/Shutterstock.com; tire mark texture used throughout Slay/Shutterstock.com; p. 5 Serg64/Shutterstock.com; p. 7 Liftarn/Wikimedia Commons; p. 9 A_Lesik/Shutterstock.com; p. 11 Jeff Schultes/Shutterstock.com; p. 13 Embedded Data Bot/Wikimedia Commons; pp. 15, 17, 21, 25 Icon Sports Wire/Contributor/Icon Sportswire/Getty Images; p. 19 Getmilitaryphotos/Shutterstock.com; p. 23 ermess/Shutterstock.com; p. 27 Matt Cardy/Stringer/Getty Images News/Getty Images; p. 29 Matt Sullivan/Stringer/Getty Images Sport/Getty Images.

Printed in the United States of America

CPSIA compliance information: Batch #CS19GS: For further information contact Gareth Stevens, New York, New York at 1-800-542-2595.

CONTENTS

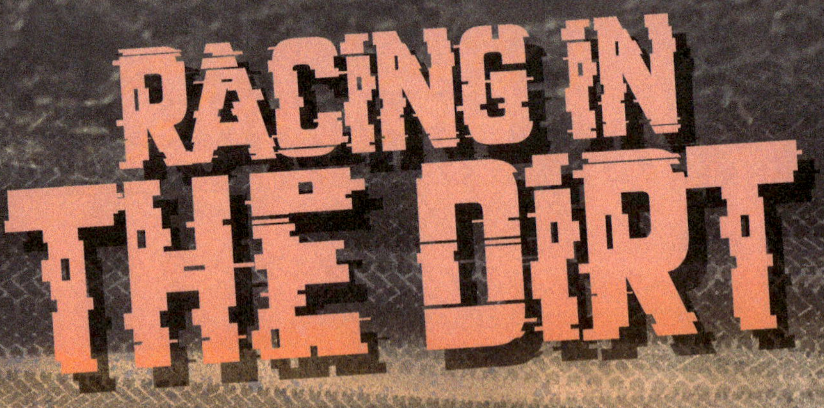

RACING IN THE DIRT

Many people love car racing. For some fans, it's all about the fast speeds and cool cars. In many races, such as in **NASCAR**, tracks are **paved**. However, that's not the case in dirt track racing. In this motorsport, the action happens on the dirt!

TEST DRIVE

AT TIMES, PAVED TRACKS HAVE BEEN COVERED IN DIRT TO BE USED FOR DIRT TRACK EVENTS!

Unlike NASCAR, dirt track racing doesn't have one big group that oversees the sport. Instead, there are many smaller groups. Because of this, rules may be different depending on the race or the track where the race is held.

TEST DRIVE

MANY OF THE GROUPS THAT GOVERN DIRT TRACK RACING ARE REGIONAL. THIS MEANS THEY ONLY OVERSEE RACES IN A CERTAIN AREA, NOT ACROSS THE COUNTRY.

RACE TO THE FINISH

Most dirt track races have multiple rounds, called heats. In each heat, drivers take several laps around the track. The number of laps depends on the size of the track. Drivers with the fastest results get to race in the main events.

TEST DRIVE

BEFORE A RACE STARTS, DRIVERS COMMONLY TAKE A FEW LAPS AROUND THE TRACK, CALLED HOT LAPS, TO MAKE SURE THEIR CARS ARE READY.

The winner of a race commonly wins some prize money. Often, there's a group of races, called a series. The top finishers of each race score points. At the end of the season, the driver with the most points wins the series!

TEST DRIVE

DIRT TRACK RACING FIRST BECAME POPULAR AROUND THE EARLY 1900S.

THE TRACK

Dirt tracks are commonly oval in shape, but they come in all different sizes. Some are only 1/8 mile (0.2 km) around. Others are 1 mile (1.6 km). Many others have a length somewhere in between.

TEST DRIVE

ON LONGER TRACKS, CARS CAN REACH FASTER SPEEDS, WHICH CAN BE DANGEROUS.

ON THE DIRT

Many dirt tracks are actually made of clay. Water is sprayed on them so they're a little sticky and don't get too dusty. Unlike paved tracks, the surface of dirt tracks can change. They can sometimes get pretty bumpy!

TEST DRIVE

TOO MUCH RAIN CAN CAUSE A RACE TO BE CANCELED BECAUSE THE TRACK WILL BE TOO MUDDY!

When racing on a paved track, cars can go through tires pretty quickly. Dirt tracks, however, are much easier on tires. A car that races on dirt tracks can usually make it through a whole season with only a few sets of tires.

TEST DRIVE

DIRT TRACK DRIVERS OFTEN HAVE A PIT CREW. THIS IS A TEAM THAT HELPS FIX THE CAR WHEN NEEDED.

MANY DIFFERENT CARS

Most dirt track races have **divisions** based on the kind of cars racing. Some cars are speedy, powerful, and heavy. Others may be smaller or have less powerful engines. It wouldn't be fair for such different cars to race against each other.

TEST DRIVE

SINCE THE CARS ARE SO DIFFERENT, THE RULES FOR EACH DIVISION ARE OFTEN DIFFERENT, TOO.

Not all cars in dirt track racing look alike. For example, open-wheel cars have no guard that covers the wheel, called a fender. Stock cars, on the other hand, look more like regular cars you'd see on the street, but have been made more powerful.

TEST DRIVE

ONE KIND OF OPEN-WHEEL CAR IS CALLED A SPRINT CAR. THESE SOMETIMES HAVE BIG WINGS ON TOP TO HELP KEEP THE CAR **STABLE**.

Some tracks have special divisions for people who are newer to racing. Often, these cars don't need to be as fancy as in other divisions. A driver can use an old car and just make some changes, such as removing all glass from the car.

TEST DRIVE

A **PROTECTIVE** FRAME CALLED A ROLL CAGE SHOULD BE ADDED TO DIRT TRACK RACING CARS TO KEEP THE DRIVER SAFE.

DANGER ON THE TRACK

Dirt track races are often less controlled than those that take place on paved courses, such as NASCAR events. Many dirt tracks in the United States don't have the same safety **barriers**, called soft walls, that bigger tracks often do.

TEST DRIVE

AT TIMES, DRIVERS HAVE DIED IN DIRT TRACK RACING. ALL KINDS OF CAR RACING CAN BE DANGEROUS, BUT DIRT TRACK RACES DON'T ALWAYS HAVE THE SAME SAFETY MEASURES THAT BIGGER RACING EVENTS HAVE.

With cars sometimes racing at speeds of more than 100 miles (160 km) per hour, crashes aren't uncommon. Safety rules all depend on the track and the group overseeing the event. Some groups require **ambulances** to be at the races!

TEST DRIVE

MANY TRACKS HAVE SOMETHING CALLED A CATCH FENCE. THIS PROTECTS THE CROWD FROM CARS OR PARTS OF CARS THAT MAY COME LOOSE DURING A CRASH.

NOT (NORMALLY) NASCAR

In the early days of NASCAR, races were often held on dirt tracks. Today, however, most NASCAR races take place on paved tracks, but not always! The Eldora Dirt Derby is a dirt track race in NASCAR's series of races for trucks.

TEST DRIVE

THE ELDORA DIRT DERBY IS HELD AT THE ELDORA SPEEDWAY IN NEW WESTON, OHIO.

DIRT TRACK RACING SAFETY TIPS

DIRT TRACK RACERS SHOULD:

- KNOW THE RULES OF THEIR RACES AND FOLLOW THEM.
- WEAR HELMETS.
- WEAR HEAD AND NECK SUPPORT DEVICES.
- HAVE ROLL CAGES IN EACH OF THEIR CARS.
- BE AWARE OF WHAT SAFETY MEASURES ARE IN PLACE AT THE TRACK THEY'RE RACING AT.
- ALWAYS KEEP THEIR BODIES INSIDE THEIR CARS.
- KNOW ABOUT THE CONDITION OF THE TRACK THEY'RE RACING ON.

FOR MORE INFORMATION

BOOKS

Bowman, Chris. *Rally Car Racing*. Minneapolis, MN: Bellwether Media, Inc., 2016.

Levit, Joe. *Motorsports Trivia: What You Never Knew About Car Racing, Monster Truck Events, and More Motor Mania.* North Mankato, MN: Capstone Press, 2019.

Weber, M. *Wild Moments of Sports Car Racing*. North Mankato, MN: Capstone Press, 2018.

WEBSITES

Bridgeport Speedway
www.bpspeedway.com/speedway-info/
Read about a speedway people call "the fastest dirt track in the East."

Dirt 101
www.onedirt.com/features/dirt-101/
Learn more about the basics and key terms having to do with dirt track racing.

How Dirt Stock Car Racing Works
auto.howstuffworks.com/auto-racing/nascar/nascar-basics/dirt-stock-car-racing.htm
Find out more about dirt track racing here.

GLOSSARY

ambulance: an automobile used to carry sick or hurt people to the hospital, often in emergencies

barrier: something that blocks movement from one place to another

division: a group of teams or people that compete against each other

NASCAR: National Association for Stock Car Auto Racing; a group that oversees stock car races in North America

paved: covered with a material that forms a hard, level surface

protective: used to keep something or someone safe

stable: not easily moved

INDEX